THE SECRET CODE BOOK

HELEN HUCKLE

THE SECRET CODE BOOK

Dial Books  New York

To Adam and Jennifer

Published by Dial Books
A Division of Penguin Books USA Inc.
375 Hudson Street
New York, New York 10014
Conceived and produced by Breslich & Foss, London
Copyright © 1995 by Breslich & Foss
All rights reserved
Printed in Hong Kong
Designed by Roger Daniels
1 3 5 7 9 10 8 6 4 2

Library of Congress Cataloging in Publication Data
Huckle, Helen.
The secret code book / Helen Huckle. — 1st ed.
p.   cm.
ISBN 0-8037-1725-3
1. Cryptography — Juvenile literature. I. Title.
Z103.3.H83   652'.8 — dc20   1995   94 - 30019   CIP

CONTENTS

PSST! WANT TO BE A SECRET AGENT?

In the 5th century an Athenian king shaved the head of a slave and tattooed a secret message onto his scalp. When the hair of the slave had grown back, the king sent the slave to deliver the message with a note, "Shave this man's head!"

During the American Revolution a traitor named Benedict Arnold sold U.S. military secrets to the British. He sent his information by using a system of numbers and scattered words in an ordinary dictionary . . . .

In the 1800's Russians who were put in prison for their political beliefs sent secret messages to one another by knocking on the walls of their cells . . . .

With *The Secret Code Book* you can join the ranks of those whose lives have been filled with adventure and excitement, mystery and intrigue. Here a wide variety of clever, fascinating, and mind-boggling codes that have been used over hundreds of years for sending vital – yet confidential – messages have been brought together. Highly creative, as well as easy to learn with the straightforward instructions included in this book, these codes involve everything from flashing lights to waving flags to hiding messages in innocent-looking letters and notes. You'll discover written languages so old they are as secretive as codes, and spoken languages like Pig Latin that are really very simple, but very tricky to figure out unless you know how! And in addition to *en*coding a message you want to send in secret, *The Secret Code Book* shows you how to figure out – decipher or *de*code – someone else's hidden one! An Answer Key at the back of the book lets you know if you're mastering the codes correctly.

The Secret Code Book is filled with surprises – even the front cover is in a code whose translation is hidden in this book – so put on your trench coat and sunglasses and get ready. . . .

SPARTAN SECRET CODES

In Greece in the 5th century B.C. the Spartan army used a special method for sending secret messages, so that the messages could only be read by the people for whom they were intended. To do this, the Spartans used a device called a *skytale* (pronounced skee-ta-lee).

The skytale was a wooden cylinder. A commander who wanted to send a message would take a long, thin strip of parchment paper and wrap it around the skytale. Then he would write the message along the length of the strip, as shown on the opposite page. When he unwound the strip, his message would unravel into a meaningless jumble of letters. This would be sent to another commander who would decipher it by winding it around a skytale of exactly the same shape and size. If an enemy got hold of it, the message would remain secret, because he would not have a skytale for deciphering it. Here are some instructions for making your own skytale. Before you begin, make sure that you have two skytales that are exactly the same size, and make sure that your friend has one before you send him or her the message, perhaps by mailing it. You could use either two wooden sticks or toilet roll tubes.

TO MAKE YOUR OWN SKYTALE

1 Cut a thin strip of paper (about half an inch across), making sure it is long enough to wind around your tube at least six times.

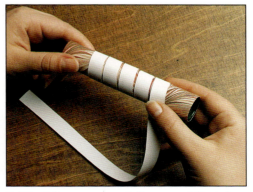

2 Wind the paper carefully around the tube as shown.

3 Write in your secret message across the tube. Fill in any spaces with nulls, letters that are just filling in blanks – usually an X or Z.

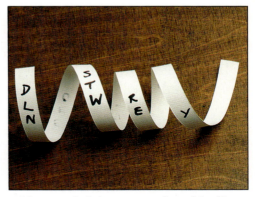

4 Now unwind the paper and send it off to your friend.

THE PIGPEN CIPHER

In the 16th century the secret society of Freemasons used a diagram cipher like this:

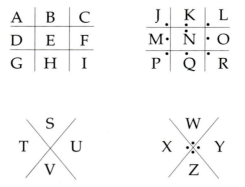

This cipher is known as the Pigpen cipher because the letters of the alphabet – the "pigs" – are trapped within the lines – the "pens." The shapes made by these "pens," either with or without a dot, represent the letters inside. So, for example:

⌐ = A , ⌐‿ = B, •⌐ = J, and ⌐• = K

•⌐ ⌐ ⌐ •⌐ ▢ ▢• = PIGPEN

Can you write the following in Pigpen?

THE MONEY IS IN THE BANK

SEND FURTHER INSTRUCTIONS

Can you figure out these hidden Pigpen messages?

A LETTER WITHIN A LETTER

Read the letter on the following page. It seems to be just an ordinary letter. But now take the first letter of each sentence and put them together. What is the message?

This is called an *open code* because the letter makes it seem as though there is nothing to hide; whereas if an obvious code is used, people will know you want to hide something! Open codes were used a lot during World War II when innocent-sounding messages would be broadcast on the radio as signs to soldiers and underground agents to put their secret plans into action. For example, when the B.B.C., the British Broadcasting Corporation, broadcast (in French) the words "It is hot in Suez," the French Resistance knew it was a signal for them to start sabotaging railroad tracks. Turn to page 36 for another type of open code.

Dear Jim,

I'm sorry I haven't written for so long. Are you feeling better? My mother told me you had a terrible cold last week. I thought I was getting the flu myself, but it seems to be gone, thank goodness.
Now that it's almost the spring, we must get together again. Nicky told me that you have gotten a great job. Everyone is so proud of you, Jim. We were all delighted that you did so well on your exams.
You certainly deserve the success. Obviously all that hard work has paid off! Really, I haven't seen you for so long that I'm not sure if I'd even recognize you! Keep up the good work.

Sincerely,
Anne

THE POLYBIUS SQUARE

Roman soldiers had a clever method of sending secret messages to each other over long distances at night. A Greek man called Polybius, who worked for the Romans, devised a system of signaling using burning torches. He drew a grid of 25 squares and wrote down one letter of the alphabet in each square (the Roman alphabet had only 25 letters. Using the English alphabet, the letters I and J must share one square in order to fit), and numbered the columns 1 to 5 across the top and down the left-hand side, like this:

	1	2	3	4	5
1	A	B	C	D	E
2	F	G	H	IJ*	K
3	L	M	N	O	P
4	Q	R	S	T	U
5	V	W	X	Y	Z

This is an example of a substitution cipher (see page 55). Each letter can be referred to as a pair of numbers, taking the number of the row first (the number on the left-hand side of the square) and the number of the column (across the top of the square) second. So, for example, the letter A becomes 1,1; the letter F becomes 2,1; and the letter P becomes 3,5.

For your signaling you will need two flashlights, one for your right hand and one for your left. Signal by turning each flashlight on and off for the number of times needed for each letter. For example, A would be one flash with your right hand and one with your left hand. P would be three with your right hand, five with your left, and so on. Make sure you leave a short break between each letter, so that the person receiving the message does not get confused. You should also make sure that he or she has two flashlights for signaling back. Before you start to signal, practice enciphering and deciphering using the square. To decipher 4,3, for example, find where row 4 meets column 3 and write down the letter, which is S.

Now try enciphering this example:

IS THERE ANY NEWS?

Now try deciphering the following example. Note that / indicates the end of a word, and // indicates the end of a sentence. It may help you to cross out each pair of numbers as you go along.

4,4, 2,3 1,5/1,5 3,3 1,5 3,2 5,4/4,3 2,3 2,4 3,5 4,3/2,3 1,1 5,1 1,5/ 1,2 1,5 1,5 3,3/4,3 2,4 2,2 2,3 4,4 1,5 1,4//3,5 4,2 1,5 3,5 1,1 4,2 1,5/4,4 3,4/2,1 2,4 2,2 2,3 4,4//

CAESAR'S SECRETS

The Roman conqueror Julius Caesar used an easy substitution cipher (see page 55) for sending his secret messages. He simply replaced each letter with the third letter after it in the alphabet, so that a = d, b = e, c = f, and so on. To use this method, you should first write out the plaintext alphabet, and then write the cipher alphabet directly underneath, like this:

PLAINTEXT

A B C D E F G H I J K L M N O P Q R S T U V W X Y Z

D E F G H I J K L M N O P Q R S T U V W X Y Z A B C

CIPHER

So Julius Caesar's famous Latin saying "Veni, Vidi, Vici," meaning "I came, I saw, I conquered," would become YHQL, YLGL, YLFL.

Now use Caesar's alphabet to encipher this message:

CAESAR IS ON HIS WAY TO THE SENATE HOUSE

Now decipher this message:

NHHS BRXU GDJJHU KLGGHQ LQ BRXU WRJD EXW SUHSDUH WR VWULNH ZKHQ L JLYH WKH VLJQDO

Right: When Caesar's enemies thought he was becoming too powerful, they plotted to kill him. This painting shows Caesar being murdered by the plotters at the Senate House.

ZIGZAG WRITING

Look at the two lines of letters below. They seem to be meaningless.

M E M T N G T

E T E O I H

Now try connecting the letters with a zigzag line, like this:

M E M T N G T

E T E O I H

The message has been written in Zigzag – the first letter up, the second letter down, the third letter up, and so on. When you write out the letters in a single line, the message reads: MEET ME TONIGHT.

A Zigzag message is written by alternating the letters of the message you want to send between the top and bottom lines, as shown above. The top line is then written out as though it is one whole word, and the second line is written as though it is another word. A dash is put between the two words, so that they look like this:

MEMTNGT – ETEOIH.

Now look at the cover of the book. The jumbled background letters, which are shown more clearly and completely on the back cover, are

actually written in Zigzag and spell out the following message: All
the codes in this book are real. They have been used by many secret
agents and spies. These codes have helped prevent disasters, save lives,
stop wars, and sometimes even start them. They took years to invent,
but they are easy to learn, and they are lots of fun!

   Can you put the messages below in Zigzag code?

ARRIVING SATURDAY

MEET ME AT THE DOCKS

   Now try to figure out these messages. (To make deciphering easier,
the letters placed on the second line should be written below the first
and slightly to the right.)

WADRCOHSNBIGTRH – ERAKLTEADRNAOC

TELNAENHCAEAKDRNE – HPASRITERTMREOAGS

SPIES AND BURIED TREASURE

During the American Revolution, Benedict Arnold (1741-1801), shown here, who was in charge of the West Point U.S. Military Academy, used a dictionary book code message (shown on page 22) when he offered to betray West Point to the British. However, any sort of book can be used for a book code. Choose a book and look through it until you have found each word of your message, and note down the page number, line number, and position on the line (e.g., 1st word, 5th word, etc.). These should be written with the page number first, followed by the line number, and then the position on that line. So if the word is the 9th one on line 15 of page 30, the code would be written like this: 30.15.9. You will need to make sure that the person who is to receive your message has a copy of the exact same book. You might, for example, use a school textbook.

Using *The Secret Code Book*, try decoding the examples given below.

36.22.3 28.9.5 12.4.6 22.2.1 48.13.9

36.20.14 8.16.8 27.7.3 49.15.5

A similar code to the one used by Benedict Arnold was used by a man named Thomas Jefferson Beale, who, in 1817, struck gold and silver in the hills 250 miles north of Santa Fe, New Mexico. After 18 months of mining, Beale had piled up a fortune, which he took back home to Virginia and hid somewhere in Bedford County. He then went back to the West and never returned. But before he left, he gave a locked box to a local innkeeper named Robert Morris, making him promise to wait 10 years, and if he had not returned, to open it. Morris waited over 20 years before he broke the lock. Inside, there was a letter that described how Beale had discovered the treasure, and three cryptograms. The letter promised that the key to the cryptograms would one day be sent to Morris, but it never arrived.

Eventually the cryptogram marked No. 2 was solved. It described the treasure, and how and when Beale had buried it, but it did not say *where* it was buried. The message ended with the words "Paper No. 1 describes the exact locality of the vault . . . ." Cryptogram No. 2 had been solved using the Declaration of Independence as the key. Beale had numbered the words of the Declaration from 1 to 1322. Each word's number stood for the first letter of that word. This was tried on the other cryptograms, but it did not work. Although many people have tried to break them by using well-known books, such as the Bible and the works of Shakespeare, no solution has ever been found .

Above: The coded message reads, "If I point out a plan of cooperation by which S[ir] H[enry Clinton] shall possess himself of West Point, the Garrison, etc., etc., twenty thousand pounds sterling I think will be a cheap purchase for an object of so much importance." (In other words, Benedict Arnold was stating that he would sell American military secrets to the British Army.)

PIG LATIN

There are many secret languages you can use with friends, and one of the easiest to learn is Pig Latin. It is very simple but when spoken can sound like a complicated foreign language. Take the first consonant sound of the word and put it at the end, then add on the syllable "ay." So "secret" becomes "ecretsay," and "third" becomes "irdthay." With a word that begins with a vowel, such as "and," simply add on "way" to the end, so that it becomes "andway." So, in Pig Latin the sentence "the quick brown fox jumps over the lazy dog" becomes "ethay ickquay ownbray oxfay umpsjay overway ethay azylay ogday."

Try "translating" these sentences into Pig Latin:

MEET ME ON THE CORNER OF THE STREET AT HALF PAST THREE

DO NOT BE LATE

Now try turning these Pig Latin sentences back into English:

IWAY ILLWAY EBAY ERETHAY

ODAY OTNAY ELLTAY ANYONEWAY ABOUTWAY OURWAY LANPAY

LANGUAGE AS CODE

We usually think of codes as something secret, but this is not always true. Sometimes a very old language becomes like a secret code because no one can understand it anymore.

Look at the pages at the front and back of this book. The symbols shown are called *hieroglyphs*. Hieroglyphs are the signs or letters used in ancient Egyptian writing. They have not been used since the 4th century B.C. and were a great puzzle for many years – until the discovery of the Rosetta Stone in 1799. This stone was carved with several different sorts

of writing, including hieroglyphs and ancient Greek writing, which the codebreakers discovered meant the same thing. Egyptian hieroglyphs are pictures of objects, people, and animals that would have been known to the ancient Egyptians. There were 24 hieroglyphs that represented the sounds of the ancient Egyptian alphabet. Some of them are given on the opposite page:

Left: Hieroglyphs from approximately 1310 B.C. The seated figure is Osiris, God of the Underworld.

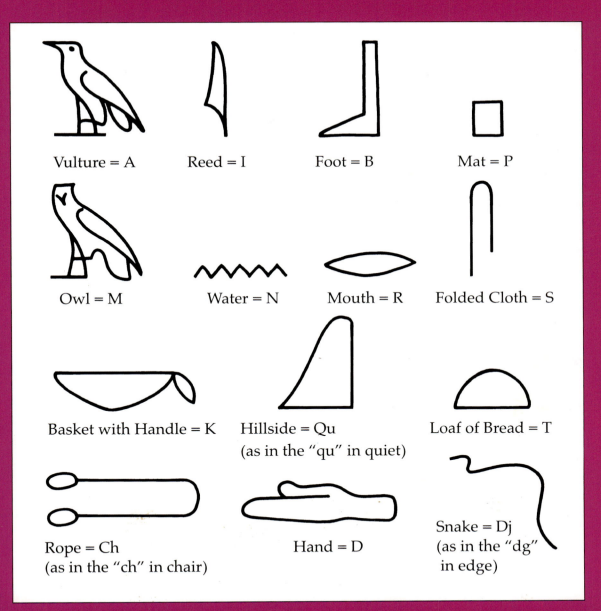

Vulture = A

Reed = I

Foot = B

Mat = P

Owl = M

Water = N

Mouth = R

Folded Cloth = S

Basket with Handle = K

Hillside = Qu
(as in the "qu" in quiet)

Loaf of Bread = T

Rope = Ch
(as in the "ch" in chair)

Hand = D

Snake = Dj
(as in the "dg"
in edge)

As well as the 24 hieroglyphs, there were some signs that represented combinations of sounds, many of which were actual Egyptian words. For example:

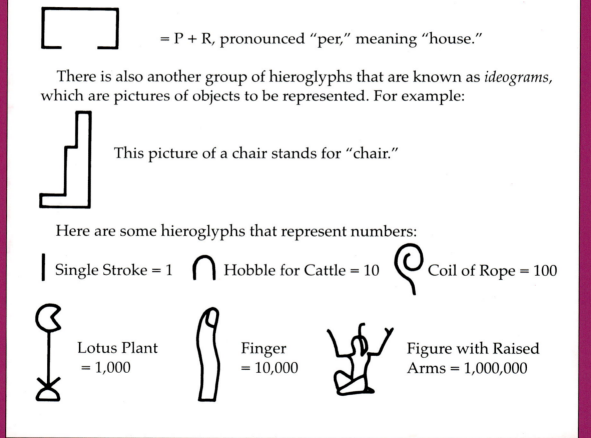

= P + R, pronounced "per," meaning "house."

There is also another group of hieroglyphs that are known as *ideograms*, which are pictures of objects to be represented. For example:

This picture of a chair stands for "chair."

Here are some hieroglyphs that represent numbers:

Single Stroke = 1   Hobble for Cattle = 10   Coil of Rope = 100

Lotus Plant = 1,000   Finger = 10,000   Figure with Raised Arms = 1,000,000

All other numbers were written down using combinations of these signs. When writing down a number in hieroglyphs, always write the higher number in front of the lower one. So, for example, the number 11 would be written ∩ | Numbers are also written in two rows.
For example, 22 would be written ∩ |
                                        ∩ |

In the case of hieroglyphs for odd numbers, which do not split into equal parts, the larger part of the number should be written on the top line. Therefore, 35 would be written   ∩ ∩ | | |
                                              ∩ | |

10 chairs would be written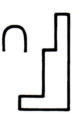

and 100 houses would be ℮ ⬓

It is also possible to make your own hieroglyphs. For example:

A chair and a desk could mean "school."

A mitt and a bat could mean "baseball."

MORSE CODE

A non-secret code known as the Morse code was devised in the 19th century by Samuel Morse, an American who had invented the electric telegraph. Morse wanted to develop a system of dots (•) and dashes (–) that would send messages along the telegraph quickly. First, he went to a newspaper printer's office so that he could see which letters in the alphabet are used the most often. He wanted these to have the signals that are quickest for people to send. He found out that E is the most common letter, followed by T, with A, I, O, and S equal in third place, followed by H. If you look at the table opposite, you will see that these particular letters have the simplest signals.

Left: Samuel Morse standing beside his code-sending machine.

A	.—	S	...
B	—...	T	—
C	—.—.	U	..—
D	—..	V	...—
E	.	W	.——
F	..—.	X	—..—
G	——.	Y	—.——
H	....	Z	——..
I	..	1	.————
J	.———	2	..———
K	—.—	3	...——
L	.—..	4	....—
M	——	5	.....
N	—.	6	—....
O	———	7	——...
P	.——.	8	———..
Q	——.—	9	————.
R	.—.	0	—————

Right: A telegraph operator on a ship sending a Morse message.

The best-known Morse code is the SOS message that is sent when people need help: ••• ━━ •••. You can transmit Morse code in different ways. Originally, it was used for messages that were sent by a series of long and short sounds down a telegraph wire, but you can do the same thing using a buzzer or an electric bell. Each dot translates as a short burst of sound, and each dash as a longer one — a dash should be equal to three dot lengths, and the time between letters should also equal three dot lengths. You could

Above and right: When the *Titanic* was sinking, this Morse message was sent: "We are sinking fast. Passengers being put into boats." The top line reads, "SOS, SOS, CQD, CQD." CQD, which stands for "Come Quick Danger," was used as the distress call before SOS — "Save Our Souls" — was introduced in 1908. When the *Titanic* sank in 1912, CQD was still used by Americans, so the radio operator who sent this message used both.

try recording your Morse code message on a cassette and then sending it to a friend to decode. You could also use a flashlight to send Morse code, flashing short bursts of light for dots, and longer ones for dashes. Decide which method you would like to use, and then try sending this message:

WHAT SHALL I DO?

   Now try decoding this message:

▬ ·· · ···   ▬ ·▬· ▬ ▬ ▬ ▬·▬▬ ·▬ ·▬·· ·▬··
▬ ·· ▬ ▬ ▬ ▬·▬· ··▬ ▬ ▬ · ▬· ▬ ···

   (If you enjoy using Morse code, it is possible to buy a little kit with a light bulb and key switch that you can assemble and use to send your messages. These kits can usually be found in most toy stores and should be put together with the help of an adult.)
   Morse code quickly became very popular; however, it was also very expensive to send, and so groups of letters were used in place of longer messages. The ACME code, for example, used in the 1920's had the following abbreviations: NARVO, Do not part with the documents; ARPUK, The person is an adventurer, have nothing to do with him; and even PYTUO, Collided with an iceberg. You can make up your own abbreviations to use with Morse code. For example, DIR could mean "Dinner is ready," or MIM could mean "Mom is mad."

HIGH-SEAS CODE

In the 18th century the British Royal Navy developed a code system using flags that is still used around the world. It is called the International Code of Signals, and it uses the flags shown opposite. Each flag represents one letter, and each smaller flag, called a pennant, represents a number. A special pennant is hung out when the ship is preparing to send out, or to answer, a message. The flags and pennants are run up on a rope and the message is read from top to bottom; the highest flag is the first part of the message.

One-letter signals are used for dire emergencies: For example, U = You are standing in danger, and O = Man overboard. Two-letter signals are distress signals: For example, NC = I need help, and AP = I am aground. A three-letter signal starting with the M flag means a medical subject: For example, MSR = Wound needs stitches. Groups of four letters show the ship's own particular signal. Each ship is issued a copy of an international code book giving the meanings of the flag codes.

You and your friends can create a similar code of your own using different colored towels and items of clothing instead of flags, and hanging them on a clothesline or waving them in order. Use larger towels or clothes such as skirts and pants to indicate meeting places. For example, a big red towel could mean "Meet at the park." Smaller towels and clothes such as socks can be used to indicate the time – a small red towel could mean "one o'clock," blue socks could mean "two o'clock," and so on.

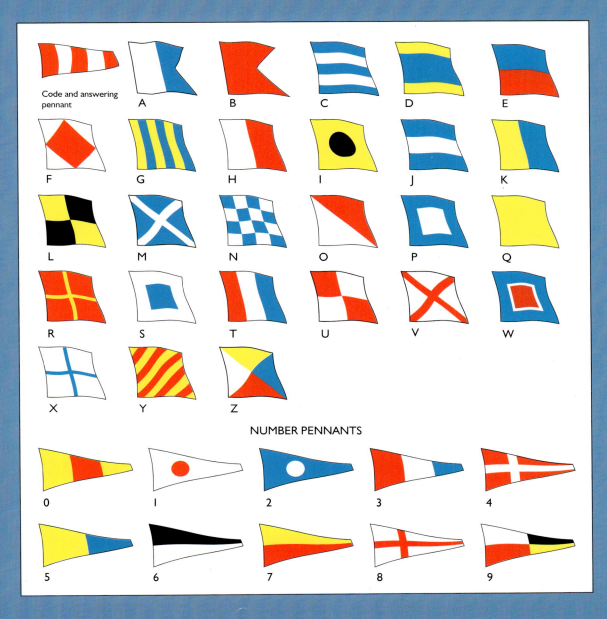

Code and answering pennant

A B C D E

F G H I J K

L M N O P Q

R S T U V W

X Y Z

NUMBER PENNANTS

0 1 2 3 4

5 6 7 8 9

SEMAPHORE

There is another international system of visual signaling with two flags called *semaphore* that used to be used by sailors for sending messages to other ships before the invention of radio. One flag is held in each hand and different body positions are taken. As shown on the opposite page, each letter of the alphabet is represented, plus a few additional meanings.

You can try sending a message to a friend using the semaphore signals. (If you don't have two flags, you can use two bandannas.) The same signals are used for letters and numbers. When you are signaling a number, use the "number" signal first, so that the person receiving does not confuse it with the corresponding letter. If you make a mistake in your signaling, you must give the "error" signal, so that the receiver will know to ignore the previous signal. At the end of your message, you must give the signal for "end," so that the receiver will know that he or she may now send a reply.

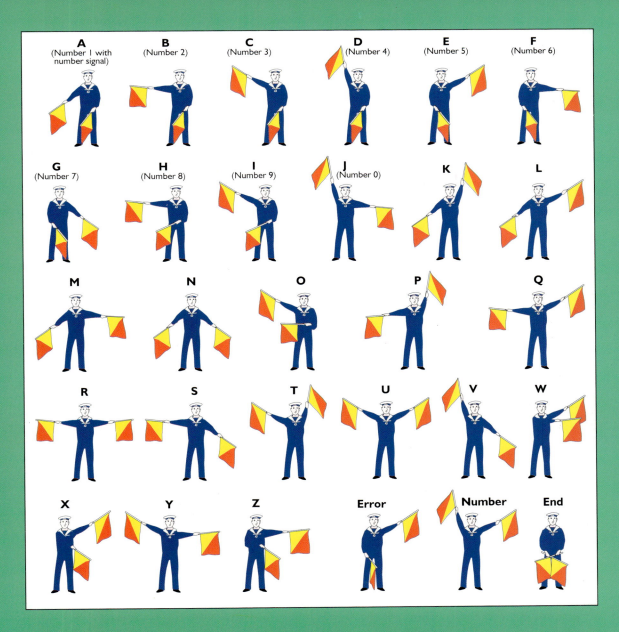

READING BETWEEN THE LINES

Read the letter on page 39. Nothing about the letter seems unusual, but this is another type of open code. By placing the attached *grille* from page 37 on top and pressing out the small rectangular holes, a hidden message is revealed. (Note that each line should be read in order.) The grille was invented in the 16th century by an Italian mathematician, Jerome Cardano. Grilles were often used by diplomats in the 16th and 17th centuries to conceal national secrets.

To make your own grille, write an ordinary letter containing the words of your secret message in different places but in the order you want them to appear in the message. Next put a piece of tracing paper over your letter and draw rectangles around the secret message words. Now transfer the squares to a piece of sturdier paper by carefully cutting out the rectangles on your tracing paper with a pair of scissors, and then putting your tracing paper on top of the sturdier piece of paper. Then outline the rectangles one more time, and finally cut out the rectangles on the sturdy piece of paper. This is now your grille.

You will need to make two of these grilles, one for yourself and one for the person to whom you are sending the letter. Be sure to give the grille to that person several days before you mail the letter, so that only *he or she* can read your secret message, in case the letter gets into anyone else's hands! In addition, if the person to whom you are sending the message wants to send back an answer, he or she can use the same grille but write a new letter!

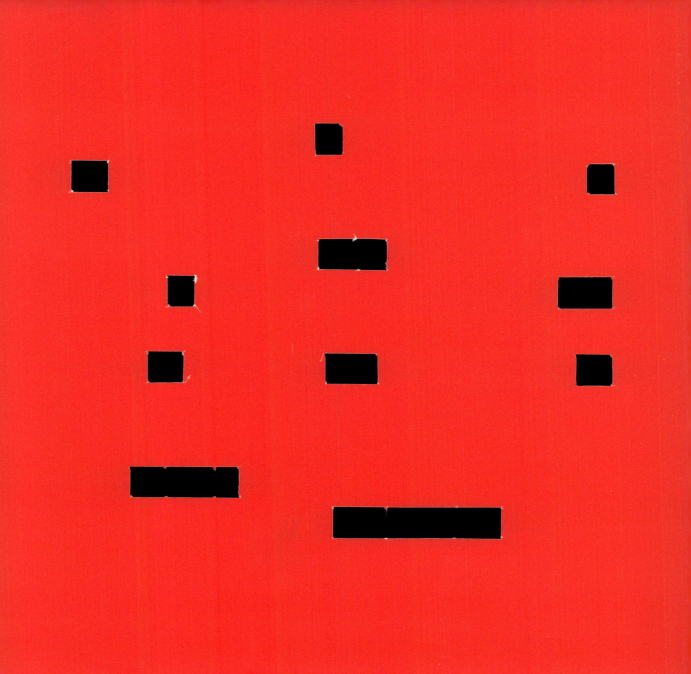

Dear Aunt Wilma,

I am sorry that I could not be with all of you
at Grandpa's birthday party, but I hope it was fun. The
weather here is terrible. It seems to be raining every
time I look out of the window. I have fixed up a little
table for myself in the shed at the bottom of the yard,
where I am studying hard for school. Dad is painting
the outside of the shed blue. Yesterday the cat next
door came to give him some help, and walked right
through the paint — paw prints everywhere! Thank you
so much for telling us about that new restaurant. We
went there on Tuesday night. It was wonderful.

Lots of love to you and Uncle Sam,
Susan

SUPERSECRETS

Using two codes or ciphers together makes your secret message even more difficult to break. This is called *superenciphering*. For example, you can use both Zigzag writing and Polybius' Square. If you use Zigzag writing (see page 18) to encipher the following message: I HAVE THE MONEY, the first cryptogram is IAEHMNY – HVTEOE. If you then encipher this message using Polybius' Square (see page 14), you get: 2,4 1,1 1,5 2,3 3,2 3,3 5,4/2,3 5,1 4,4 1,5 3,4 1,5. To decipher the final cryptogram, you go "in reverse" by using Polybius' Square to get the letters, and then rewriting these letters in the zigzag pattern to get the plaintext message. Using Zigzag and Polybius' Square, try superenciphering the following message. (Again, it may be helpful to cross out the numbers as you go along.)

WHAT SHALL I DO?

Now try deciphering this message. (A reminder: A double slash / / indicates the end of a sentence. It is easier to decipher one sentence at a time rather than "translating" all the numbers to letters at once.)

3,5 4,4 2,3 3,2 3,3 5,4 3,3 4,3 2,4 1,3 4,3/4,5 4,4 1,5 3,4 1,5 2,4 1,1
4,5 4,4 1,1 1,5//4,4 2,5 2,4 4,4 4,4 1,5 4,4 4,4 3,4/1,1 1,5 4,4 3,4 2,3
4,3 1,1, 2,4 3,3//3,1 1,1 1,5 4,4 3,3 4,5 2,2 2,2 3,1 1,3 1,5 4,4 4,2
1,5/1,5 5,1 2,4 2,4 3,1 2,2 1,1 1,5 3,4 2,5 4,2 2,3 1,5//1,4 3,3 4,4
3,1 4,4 1,5 3,4 2,4 1,5/3,4 4,4 1,5 3,1 2,3 3,5 3,1 1,3//

The following cryptogram was enciphered by first using Zigzag and then the Pigpen Cipher (see page 10):

PLAINTEXT: LEAVE TONIGHT

ZIGZAG: LAEOIH-EVTNGT

PIGPEN CIPHER: ⌊• ⌋□•⌈⊓—□∧>•⌐>

Here are some messages that have been superenciphered using the same method. See if you can decipher them:

⌈⌈⌊•□<•⊓⌊•>□∨⊓•⊓∧>□•⊏□—∨⌊•⌈
>⌈•>□□>⌈•∨□⌈⌋□⊓•⌋•<

>□⌈⌊•>⌈⌊•□□⊓⊣⌐⊏□⊏•>⌋>□>>⊏—⊓>
⌊□∨⌊•⌊⌈>□⊓•⌣⊏⊓>⊓∨⌋⌈•

Now try using combinations of different methods to create your own superencipherments.

THE KNOCKING NIHILISTS

In 19th-century Russia many people were put in prison for their political beliefs. Since very often they were separated from one another, they developed a way of "talking" to each other by knocking on the walls of their cells, using a certain number of knocks for each letter. The numbers were determined by a checkerboard diagram like Polybius' Square (see page 14).

For example, WELCOME would be 5,2 1,5 3,1 1,3 3,4 3,2 1,5. So if you want to send the message "Welcome," you would knock five times with your left hand, pause slightly, and then knock twice with your right for W, once with your left hand and five times with your right for E, and so on, leaving a small space between "letters" so that the listener does not get confused.

The prisoners learned the substituted numbers by heart, and some of them could "talk" to each other at the rate of 10 or 15 words per minute. One group of prisoners, called the Nihilists, used this cipher as a basis for a more complicated one. First, they converted the plaintext message into numbers according to the checkerboard, and then they chose a repeating keyword that they also converted into numbers. Then they added the two sets of numbers together to make the final cipher. For example, using the word PRISON as the repeating keyword, which

Right: A Russian poster. The large man with the banner walking through the streets of Moscow was a symbol of the Communist revolution that swept across Russia at the beginning of this century.

enciphers as 3,5 4,2 2,4 4,3 3,4 3,3, the plaintext STORM THE PALACE would be enciphered as follows:

PLAINTEXT:	S T O R M	T H E	P A L A C E
NUMBERS FROM PLAINTEXT:	43 44 34 42 32	44 23 15	35 11 31 11 13 15
NUMBERS FROM KEYWORD:	35 42 24 43 34	33 35 42	24 43 34 33 35 42
	78 86 58 85 66	77 58 57	59 54 65 44 48 57

Try enciphering this message, still using PRISON as the keyword:

BLOW UP THE TSAR

To decipher, write down the enciphered message, and then write the numbers of the key beneath them, like this (still using PRISON):

CRYPTOGRAM:	79 57 55 74 88 67 80 84 37 77 66 75 46 56 39 86
NUMBERS FROM KEYWORD:	35 42 24 43 34 33 35 42 24 43 34 33 35 42 24 43

Then subtract the "key" numbers from the cryptogram numbers, and you will have the numbers of the original message: 44 15 31 31 54 34 45 42 13 34 32 42 11 14 15 43. You can then look these up on the checkerboard diagram. They should read: TELL YOUR COMRADES.

Now try deciphering this one (again using PRISON):

78 86 35 85 78 / 77 58 57 / 66 58 85 67 66 87 68 67 68 66

THOMAS JEFFERSON'S CIPHER

Thomas Jefferson (1743-1826) was the third president of the United States and also a great inventor. Before he became president, he invented a "cypher wheel," which basically worked like a combination lock. The original machine was a row of wheels held through their centers by a rod so that each wheel could turn separately from the others, and be fixed at particular points. Around the outside of each wheel the alphabet was printed, but the order of the letters would be jumbled. The message was enciphered by turning each wheel until the correct letters appeared all in one row, forming the plaintext. The ciphertext could be any other row the sender chose, and he or she would write this down and send it. The person who received the message would then get his or her own machine, move the wheels around until one row showed the ciphertext, and then look for the row that showed the plaintext.

If you want to use Thomas Jefferson's method, you should make two cipher machines exactly the same – one for you and one for a friend. Turn the page for instructions on how to make a machine like the one shown. You will need a soft-drink can, a blank sheet of white paper, a pen, a pair of scissors, and some sticky tape.

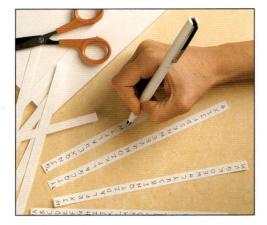

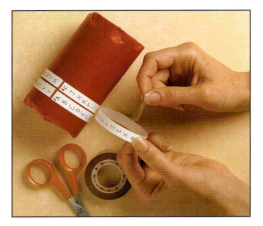

1 Take the sheet of paper, and cut 10 equal strips. Divide these into 26 equal sections and write the following alphabets on the different strips, with each letter on top of the next so that they read downward. Number each strip as you go to avoid confusion.

2 Tape the ends of each strip together to make loops. Slide each loop in turn over one end of the can in the order listed below.

```
Strip  1: A B C D E F G H I J K L M N O P Q R S T U V W X Y Z
Strip  2: F J X R P L A D Z T Q N I B S U Y C H W E O K G V M
Strip  3: Y T Q C G A L P K Z O M U V B E W N R S D F J I X H
Strip  4: G J N Q X E U A L P T W M I O K R Z V F C Y S H B D
Strip  5: D T J O H A Y V U R Q L B F K N W P Z C E G X S M I
Strip  6: U C T H M D O Y N X L Q W Z I G B P F V E R S A K J
Strip  7: K P M B L X J Y W A Z E Q V U S D N I T H G F C R O
Strip  8: X G Z L Q C T R W N J A D I E S V B F O H M Y P U K
Strip  9: E W I L C R J O H A T Z Q S U V F N K X G D Y M B P
Strip 10: Q X K S U I F T L O G C P W Z B N Y R E H A M J V D
```

Repeat steps 1 and 2 so you have a cipher to give to a friend to read your secret message. (Remember that the alphabets on both cans must be in the same order.) With your cipher machine, try enciphering the following: REPORT BACK. In this case, use the row directly *above* the plaintext to provide the cryptogram, which should read QWLIUC MJLX. See if your friend can figure out the message.

Now try enciphering these messages, using the row directly *beneath* the plaintext as the cryptogram:

ENEMY AGENT

ALIAS SMITH

OPERATING (Note: Since the word "operating" has only 9 letters, you will have to use a null at the end – OPERATINGX.)

Now try deciphering the message below. Because of its length, it has been divided into three parts. First arrange the strips so that these letters are spelled out in a row, and then look at the rows above and below until you find one that makes sense. That will be the plaintext message.

VXYIVPIESU   JAKEOOMNLC   RSXZLKFPFG

(These are all in the third row above the cryptogram.)

CIPHER DISK

The cipher disk was invented by an Italian named Leon Battista Alberti in the 15th century. His invention led him to be known as the "father of Western cryptology." Alberti knew that a secret message would be very hard for someone to figure out if several alphabets were used, so he created a disk where every letter in the regular alphabet is replaced by another letter. Alberti's disk has been adapted and used in a variety of forms, such as the cipher slide and cipher table.

To make your own cipher disk, turn to the back of the book and press out one large and one small disk. Put the small disk on top of the larger one (with both facing you) and center them on the tip of a pencil so that they can be spun around. The big disk is for the regular – plaintext – alphabet, and the small one for the cipher alphabet.

Next, a keyword is needed. Using the keyword LEMON to encode the message BURN THE PAPERS, you must first write the word LEMON repeatedly under the message, like this:

BURN THE PAPERS
LEMO NLE MONLEM

The keyword shows that you need to encipher the first letter of the message, B, using the L alphabet. To get this alphabet, spin the disk around until the L on the cipher alphabet (smaller disk) is directly below the A on the plaintext (larger) disk. Now find B on your plaintext disk, and write down the cipher letter directly beneath it (M). To encipher the next letter of the message, U, you need to use the E alphabet. Spin the disk until E is directly below A, then look for U on the plaintext alphabet and write down the letter directly beneath it (Y). If you carry on in this way until you have enciphered the whole sentence, the result should read: MYDB GSI BOCPVE.

In order to decipher the message, you need to know the keyword – in this case, LEMON – and then reverse the process, as follows: To decipher M, use the L cipher alphabet. Turn the cipher disk until its L is under the plaintext A. Then look for M on the cipher disk, and write down the plaintext letter above it (B). Continue until you have deciphered the whole message.

Still using the keyword LEMON, try using your cipher disk to encipher the following messages:

I AM BEING FOLLOWED

GO INTO HIDING

Now use the keyword PARSLEY to decipher these messages:

NOLJ NSTTR ZK MPMLN

SO EGE VCIUIF

To send an enciphered message to a friend, send them the other disks at the back of this book. Then send your hidden message and a keyword.

THE TURNING GRILLE

During World War I "turning grilles" were used to switch around the order of the letters of messages that had to be sent in secret.

Turning grilles must be square, like the one shown here, but they can be many different sizes: 25, 36, 49, 64, 81, or 100 squares. During the war the sizes were given code names such as Anna for a 25-square grille and Franz for a 100-square grille, so that the person receiving the message would know which grille to use in deciphering it.

To make a 36-square turning grille, take a piece of cardboard and draw a square box 4 inches by 4 inches. Now divide it into 36 squares, and cut out the squares that match the white squares shown here. It is important that when the grille is placed in each of its four positions, no square beneath the grille should be "open" at the same place more than once. Label the sides 1 through 4 as shown here.

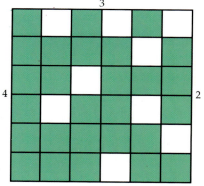

Next you must choose a message. First try the following example: LEAVE HERE TOMORROW, TELL NO ONE, GOOD LUCK. The message can only have as many letters as there are squares. If the message is "in between" sizes, nulls should be used to make it work out. This example has 34 letters, so 2 null letters will be needed. Always put nulls at the ends of words, not in the middle. (LEAVE HERE TOMORROWX TELL NO ONE GOOD LUCKX). Now place your grille on a piece of paper and draw around it in pencil so that you can reposition it easily. First position your grille with the number 1 at the bottom. Then begin writing the message inside the cut-out squares, going from left to right and following each line down as you would for normal writing. When you have filled all the squares with the grille in the first position, rotate it through 90 degrees to the right so that side 2 is now at the bottom and continue writing the message inside the cut-out squares. Rotate and repeat for sides 3 and 4 to complete the message. When you remove the grille, it should look like the square of letters to the right.

```
G L T E O A
E O T D V O
L L E M L U
O H C N E R
K O R X O R
O W N E E X
```

You can then write it out as GLTEOAEOTDVOLLEMLUOHCNER KORXOROWNEEX so it is even more confusing to everyone but the person you want to have decipher it. You should make sure that they have exactly the same grille, perhaps by sending it to them separately. Then he or she can arrange the letters in six groups of six, as above, and using the grille in the original order, can decipher it.

Using the same grille, try enciphering this message:

WAIT IN THE BACKYARD UNTIL I GIVE THE SIGNAL

And deciphering this one:

OTNHGEDKIEKDNTEDHNEYEEINLOBXESLHDHDI

THE ENIGMA MACHINE

During World War II certain machines were used that could encipher messages mechanically. These were very helpful because during the First World War all enciphering had been done by hand and a lot of mistakes were made. The Enigma machine, shown right, was a machine of this type used by the German army. As you can see, it looks like a typewriter with two different keyboards – one alphabet for the plaintext and one for the enciphering text. The plaintext keyboard was wired up to "rotors" or cipher wheels inside the machine, which, in turn, were wired to the cipher keyboard. When a plaintext key was pressed, the rotors inside gave the cipher for that letter, and that letter would light up on the cipher keyboard. So if, for example, the cipher for A was P, then when plaintext letter A was pressed, cipher letter P would light up. One could then simply write down the letters of the ciphered text and send the message. The person who received the message would type the cipher letters on the cipher keyboard and the corresponding letters would light up on the plaintext keyboard, revealing the original message. It was thought to be impossible to break the Enigma cryptograms, but after months of work a team of British mathematicians managed to do so.

To make two simple Enigma machines – one for you and one for a friend – you will need two soft-drink cans, four strips of paper, a pair of scissors, and a pen. If you have already made Thomas Jefferson's cipher (page 45), then you can simply remove all the loops of paper from the soft-drink can except for the basic alphabet, and the one next to it (Strips 1 and 2). If not, follow the instructions on page 46, but make and use Strips 1 and 2 only. You should fix Strip 1 firmly in place around the can so that it cannot be moved, but the other strip should be fixed loosely, as on Thomas Jefferson's cipher. Strip 1 is the plaintext strip and Strip 2 is the cipher strip. To use this cipher, you should first set two "keyletters," one on each of the strips, and make sure they are placed side by side. To encipher the word ENIGMA using the keyletters KD, do the following:

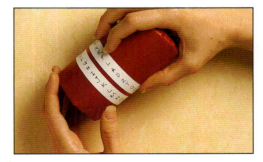

1 Find the letter K on Strip 1, and move Strip 2 so that D is next to the K.

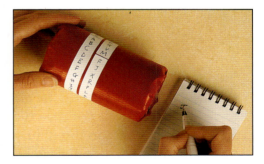

2 To encipher E, find the letter E on Strip 1 and write down the corresponding letter on Strip 2, which is J.

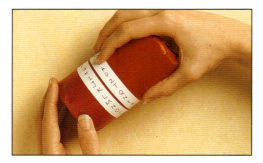

3 Move Strip 2 one letter space forward (away from you), so that K is now opposite Z.

4 To encipher N, find the letter N on Strip 1 and write down the corresponding letter on Strip 2, which is N. Continue this for the rest of the word, moving Strip 2 one letter space forward for each new plaintext letter.

The enciphered word should read JNDABX. Now try enciphering this message using the keyletters AQ:

YOUR SECRET IS SAFE WITH ME

To decipher a message, you need to know which keyletters were used. Move the cipher strip around until the keyletters are together, and then find the first letter of the cryptogram on the cipher strip. Find the corresponding letter on the plaintext strip and write it down. Then move the cipher strip forward by one letter space, find the next cipher, and write down the corresponding plaintext letter. Continue this until you have the whole message.

Try deciphering this message, using the keyletters JR:

ZZDO V LPSQGK DAE TFSNK AOGZ WAKV

GLOSSARY

Cipher: Letters, numbers, or signs that are used to replace the letters of a message one wants to conceal. A cipher that mixes up the order of the letters is a *transposition cipher,* and a cipher that replaces them with numbers, symbols, or other letters is a *substitution cipher.*

Code: A system of words, numbers, or signs that stand in place of whole words.

Cryptography: From the Greek words *crypton* meaning "hidden" and *graphos* meaning "writing." It means any method of altering the original plaintext message by encoding or enciphering it. An enciphered message is often called a *cryptogram.*

Decipher/Decode: To turn an enciphered or encoded message back into the original plaintext message.

Encipher/Encode: To turn a plaintext message into a cipher or code.

Key: Just like the key to a door, a keyword, keyphrase, or keynumber helps in concealing or figuring out a message.

Null: A meaningless letter used in a secret message. It is normally a little-used letter of the alphabet such as X or Z. It is used either to make up the correct number of letters for a certain cipher, or to confuse someone trying to break the code.

Plaintext: The original message that one wants to conceal, by encoding or enciphering it. The plaintext alphabet is the alphabet from A to Z with all the letters in their normal order.

ANSWER KEY

p.11

>⊓□ ⊒⊑□□< ⌐∨ ⌐□ >⊓□ ⨄⌐□⨅

∨□□⌐ ⊑<⌐>⊓□⌐ ⌐□∨>⌐<⌐⌐□□∨

MAIL ME ONE HUNDRED DOLLARS.
THE PARCEL ARRIVES TONIGHT.

p.13

I AM IN NEW YORK.

p.15

2,4 4,3/ 4,4 2,3 1,5 4,2 1,5/ 1,1 3,3 5,4/
3,3 1,5 5,2 4,3?
THE ENEMY SHIPS HAVE BEEN SIGHTED.
PREPARE TO FIGHT.

p.16

FDHVDU LV RQ KLV ZDB WR WKH
VHQDWH KRXVH
KEEP YOUR DAGGER HIDDEN IN YOUR
TOGA, BUT PREPARE TO STRIKE WHEN I
GIVE THE SIGNAL.

p.19

ARVNSTRA – RIIGAUDY
MEMATEOK – ETETHDCS
WEAR DARK CLOTHES AND BRING A
TORCH.
THE PLANS ARE IN THE CRATE MARKED
ORANGES.

p.20

SHE IS CODE NAMED LEMON.
GIVE HIM THE PARSLEY.

p.23

EETMAY EMAY ONWAY ETHAY
ORNERCAY OFWAY ETHAY EETSTRAY
ATWAY ALFHAY ASTPAY EETHRAY
ODAY OTNAY EBAY ATELAY
I WILL BE THERE.
DO NOT TELL ANYONE ABOUT OUR
PLAN.

p.31

•— ••• •- — / ••• ••••
•— •—•• •—•• / •• / —••
——— ?

DESTROY ALL DOCUMENTS.

p.39

BE AT THE WINDOW TABLE OF THE BLUE
CAT RESTAURANT ON TUESDAY NIGHT.

p.40

WASALD – HTHLIO
5,2 1,1 4,3 1,1 3,1 1,4/2,3 4,4 2,3 3,1 2,4 3,4

PTHMNYNSICS – UTEOEIAUTAE
TKITTETTO – AETOHSAIN
LAETNUGGLCETRE – EVIILGAEOKRHE
DNTLTEOIE – OTELHPLC
PUT THE MONEY IN A SUITCASE. TAKE IT
TO THE STATION. LEAVE IT IN LUGGAGE
LOCKER THREE. DON'T TELL THE POLICE.

p.41
IILEUNHLTESHNHVTEOE –
WLRTRTEETRWEIAEHMNY
I WILL RETURN THE LETTERS WHEN I
HAVE THE MONEY.

TEIKTILENHPOEOTATETTO –
HTCEWLBITEHNBOHTHSAIN
THE TICKET WILL BE IN THE PHONE
BOOTH AT THE STATION.

p.44
47 73 58 95 / 79 68 / 79 65 39 / 87 77 44 77
START THE REVOLUTION

p.47
FIWIV KFSKL
BAXLM ABEZA
PLWZYHTJDK
SMITH IS AT
GRAND HOTEL
ON FOURTH ST.

p.49
T EY PRTRS TDWPAKRO
RS UBGZ LURVYK
YOUR COVER IS BLOWN.
DO NOT RETURN.

p.51
TWNAHITEBSTAIIICLGKNNITYAGALRHI
DVEEU
THE KEY IS HIDDEN BEHIND THE OLD
DOG KENNEL.

p.54
ZMAP AWHZKI XB SGRR KTOQ YT
ONLY A GENIUS CAN BREAK THIS CODE.

Acknowledgments

Bridgeman Art Library, p.17; National
Portrait Gallery, Smithsonian Institution /
Art Resource, p.20; William L. Clements
Library, University of Michigan, Ann Arbor,
p.21; British Museum, London , p. 24 and
endpapers; Museum of the City of New
York, p. 28; Novosti, p. 43; Imperial War
Museum, London, p.52.

Illustrations on pp. 25, 26, 27, and 50 by King
& King
Illustrations on pp. 33 and 35 by Tony
Garrett
Photography on pp. 8, 9, 45, 46, 53, and 54 by
Visuel 7